Jolly

Grammar

Glossary

A

abstract noun

An abstract noun is a **noun** (a 'thing') that cannot be experienced through the five senses. Abstract nouns can be ideas (such as 'justice' or 'freedom'), feelings (such as 'anger' or 'happiness'), qualities (such as 'kindness' or 'bravery'), actions and events (such as 'a walk', 'a meeting' or 'a dance').

Many abstract nouns are formed by adding a suffix, such as ‹-ness›, to an adjective or a verb, as in the word 'kind**ness**'.

accent

Accent refers to the way in which the words of a language are pronounced by a particular person or a particular group of people. Typically, people's accents vary depending on where they come from.

Accent is distinct from dialect, which refers to the variety of language, including vocabulary and grammar, used by a particular person or a particular group of people.

active voice

The active voice is used when the noun, pronoun or noun phrase that 'does' the action of the verb is also the subject of that verb. For example, in the sentence 'The hamster bit the boy', the hamster is both the subject of the verb and the noun that is 'doing' the biting; this sentence uses the active voice.

However, in the sentence 'The boy was bitten by the hamster', the boy appears as the subject of the sentence, but he is on the receiving end of the verb action (the biting); this sentence uses the passive voice. The active voice is far more common than the passive voice.

adjective

An adjective describes (or 'modifies') a noun or a pronoun. Adjectives can be used directly before the noun, as in 'the **red** car' (the 'attributive' position), or elsewhere in the sentence, as in 'the car was **red**' (the 'predicate' position). Adjectives are commonly found after the verb 'be', as its complement, as in 'be nice'.

Sometimes, a word that is usually a different part of speech can act as an adjective: for example, in 'rabbit hutch' the first noun, 'rabbit', is acting as an adjective and describing the second noun, 'hutch'. Similarly, in the phrase 'the running water', the present participle, 'running' is describing the noun 'water'. Possessive nouns always act as adjectives: for example, 'the **peacock's** tail' or 'the **dog's** ball'.

In English, we tend to write adjectives in a certain order: with determiners (such as 'the') first, followed by opinions (such as 'good'), size and shape adjectives (such as 'small' or 'square'), condition and age adjectives (such as 'broken' or 'new'), colour and pattern adjectives (such as 'blue' or 'stripy'), origin (such as 'Japanese' or 'European') and, finally, material (such as 'wooden' or 'leather') before writing the noun. So, we would write "the good little blue bike" rather than "the blue little good bike". This is only a general rule and sometimes the order changes; for example, when shape and age are both included in a description, age tends to come before shape, as in 'the old square box'.

adverb

An adverb describes (or 'modifies') a verb or a verb phrase. Adverbs often describe how, where, when, how much or how often something happens and many take the suffix <-ly> (as in 'slowly'). These types of adverbs are called adverbs of manner, place, time, degree and frequency.

As well as describing verbs, adverbs can also modify adjectives (as in '**very** happy') or other adverbs (as in '**really** quickly').

adverbial

An adverbial is any word, phrase or clause that acts like an adverb within a sentence. An adverbial does not necessarily have to include an adverb: prepositional phrases, non-finite verb phrases, adverbial clauses and noun phrases (bare-NP adverbials) can all act as adverbs. For example, in the sentence 'The man walked **up the mountain**', the prepositional phrase 'up the mountain' is an adverbial, modify-ing the verb 'walked'. Similarly, in the sentence 'We went **to feed the ducks**', the non-finite verb phrase 'to feed the ducks' modifies the verb 'went'; and in the sentence 'We leave this week', the noun phrase 'this week' modifies the verb 'leave'.

Adverbials can express time, telling us when something happens ('this Wednesday', 'next year', 'yesterday morning'), how often it happens ('every time', 'each winter'), or how long it takes ('all afternoon', 'the whole day').

Other adverbials can modify the verb in a range of ways, most commonly telling us more about how ('loudly', 'without complaint'), where ('in the house', 'wherever I go'), when ('during the week', 'after we had eaten'), or why ('for their wedding anniversary', 'because it was raining').

adverbial clause

An adverbial clause is a type of subordinate clause that acts like an adverb within a sentence. For example, in the sentence 'When I have finished my book, I will go for a run', the adverbial clause 'When I have finished my book' modifies the verb 'will go'. Adverbial clauses can describe how, where, when, how much or how often something happens.

affix

An affix is a type of morpheme. An affix that is added to the beginning of a word is called a prefix, and an affix that is added to the end of a word is called a suffix.

alliteration

Alliteration is the term for the repetition of an initial consonant sound in a number of words in a sentence. For example, in the sentence 'Little Lucy Lawson leapt lightly over the lazy lamb lying in the lane,' the consonant /l/ is the initial sound in almost every word. Alliterative sentences are very common in poetry.

ambiguity

Ambiguity occurs when a single word, phrase or sentence has two or more distinctly different meanings. For example, 'Duck!' could mean 'Look, there's a duck', or it could be an order to bend down quickly so as to avoid a missile. Similarly, the sentence 'Mabel likes chocolate more than Thomas' could mean that Mabel likes chocolate more than Thomas likes chocolate, or it could mean that Mabel likes chocolate more than she likes Thomas. The sentence 'The fish was off' also has two possible meanings: the fish (animal) suddenly swam away, or the fish (food stuff) was rotten.

antonym

'Antonym' is another word for 'opposite'. Common antonym pairs include 'good' and 'bad', 'high' and 'low', and 'fast' and 'slow'.

See also synonym.

apostrophe

An apostrophe (') is used with the letter ‹s› after a noun to indicate possession of another noun: for example, 'Felicity's bag', 'the dog's ball' and 'Dad's pen'. When forming a possessive plural, we omit the ‹s› after the apostrophe, so we get 'the boys' socks' and 'the trees' leaves' (rather than 'the boys's socks' and 'the trees's leaves').

An apostrophe can also be used in a contraction to show where letters have been omitted: for example 'isn't' ('is not'), 'they'll' ('they will'), 'haven't' ('have not') and 'can't' (cannot).

appositive

An appositive is a noun or noun phrase that comes immediately after another noun or noun phrase and refers to the same person, place or thing. The two noun phrases are said to be 'in apposition'.

A restrictive appositive is a noun phrase that is necessary for the identification of the first noun. For example, in the sentence 'My friend Joe plays the guitar', the appositive, 'Joe', is necessary to clarify and limit the first noun phrase 'my friend': I have more than one friend and without the name there would be no way of knowing which of my friends plays the guitar.

A nonrestrictive appositive is not necessary for the identification of the first noun; it simply provides some more information about it. For example, in the sentence 'I lived in Oxford, a beautiful city, for just over a year', the appositive 'a beautiful city' is not necessary; it is simply my opinion about the city, and the sentence would still make sense without it. Nonrestrictive appositives are usually separated from the rest of the sentence by a pair of commas, as in the example above.

article

The words 'a', 'an' and 'the' are known as articles. The articles are determiners, which are themselves special types of adjectives. The articles 'a' and 'an' are used before singular nouns (as in '**a** man' or '**an** egg') and are called the indefinite articles. The word 'the' is used before singular and plural nouns (as in '**the** dog' or '**the** boys') and is called the definite article.

aspect (verbs)

While a verb's tense tells us when the action (or state) takes place, the aspect tells us whether that action continues over time (the continuous aspect), is repeated or habitual, or is a distinct, completed action (the perfect aspect). For example, the sentences 'I **was running**' and 'I **had run**' both take place in the past, but they have different aspects: 'I **was running**' is in the continuous aspect (also known as the 'progressive' aspect) and 'I **had run**' is in the perfect aspect.

Aspect and tense are often conflated and, for simplicity, we avoid using the term 'grammatical aspect' when teaching children about verbs and verb tenses in the Jolly Phonics grammar programme. Instead, we refer to the various tenses in the continuous aspect as the 'continuous tenses', and the various tenses in the perfect aspect as the 'perfect tenses'.

auxiliary verb

An auxiliary verb is a 'helping verb'. Auxiliary verbs are usually used together with a main verb, and tell us about the tense, aspect or mood of that main verb. The most common auxiliary verbs are 'to be' and 'to have': for example, 'We are playing' and 'We have played'. 'Will' and 'shall' are common modal auxiliaries, and help to show the future: for example, 'We shall play.'

Unlike other verbs, auxiliary verbs can be negated. So, while we can say 'He will not run' or 'He won't run', we cannot say 'He not run'.

B

bare infinitive (verbs)

When the infinitive form of the verb is used without the word 'to' in front of it, it is known as the bare infinitive.

blending

To 'blend' means to run together two or more letter sounds in order to form words (or parts of words): for example, we run together the letter sounds /f/, /l/, /a/, /g/ in order to form the word 'flag'. Blending is sometimes referred to as 'synthesising', and is the first strategy for reading unknown words when literacy is taught using a synthetic phonics approach.

brackets

(see parentheses)

bullet

A bullet (•) is sometimes used before each item in a vertical list (a list in which each item is shown on a new line, underneath the previous item).

C

capital letter

A capital letter (such as 'A', 'B', 'C' or 'D') is used at the beginning of a sentence: for example, 'The dog is sleeping.' We also use a capital letter at the beginning of a proper noun: for example, 'Tuesday', 'Jim', 'Mr Evans', 'November', 'Asia', 'Toronto'. Proper adjectives, which come from proper nouns, also have capital letters at the beginning: for example, 'Irish', 'British', 'Indian', 'Spanish' and 'Vietnamese'. Lastly, the personal pronoun 'I' is always written with a capital letter.

Unlike the lower-case letters, the capital letters should not be joined up when writing.

clause

A clause is a group of words that contains a verb and a subject and makes sense. A main (or 'independent') clause can stand alone as a sentence. For example, the main clause 'I bought some shoes' works as a complete sentence by itself.

A subordinate (or 'dependent') clause must be used together with a main clause as part of a complex (or compound-complex) sentence. For example, the subordinate clause 'While he was at the bank' does not work as a complete sentence by itself. We are left wondering what happened while he was at the bank. It is only when it is used with a main clause that it forms a complete sentence, as in the complex sentence 'While he was at the bank, I bought some shoes.'

See also adverbial clause, complement clause, dependent clause, independent clause, main clause and subordinate clause.

cloze activity

A cloze activity is a piece of text that has had some of the words removed. Cloze activities can be used to test vocabulary and comprehension skills, as the child needs these to fill in the gaps.

cohesion

Cohesion refers to the linking of words and sentences within a piece of text so as to bring coherence, unity and clarity of meaning. Cohesive devices are used to promote cohesion.

cohesive device

Cohesive devices are used to link words and sentences within a piece of text so as to bring coherence, unity and clarity of meaning.

Pronouns, determiners, conjunctions, adverbs and ellipsis can all be used as cohesive devices. Pronouns and determiners promote cohesion by referring to the nouns or noun phrases used earlier. For example, in 'Helen read Jane Eyre. **She** liked **the** book very much', the pronoun 'she' refers back to 'Helen' and the definite article 'the' (a determiner) refers back to the particular book.

Conjunctions and adverbs can be used to clarify time relationships, or indicate cause and effect. For example, in 'The children had ice-cream **while** they were walking home. **Consequently**, they are not hungry now', the conjunction 'while' makes the time relationship between the first two clauses clear, and the adverb 'consequently' indicates that the children's lack of hunger is due to their earlier consumption of ice-cream.

Ellipsis involves missing out words or phrases that have already been said, as in the conversation 'Did Mary reply to the email?' 'No, she didn't.' The words 'reply to the email' are omitted from the response. This promotes cohesion because it clearly links the response to the question.

collective noun

Collective nouns describe a group (or 'collection') of people, animals or things: for example, 'a **crowd** of people', 'a **flock** of birds' and 'a **fleet** of ships'. They can also describe abstract nouns (as in 'a **host** of ideas').

colon

A colon (:) is used to introduce a list, as in the sentence, 'Jonny squashed everything he owned into his bag: clothes, shoes, books, pens, a tennis racket and the kitchen sink.'

A colon can also be used before a definition or an explanation, as in the following sentences, 'Today, we learnt about the rhinoceros: a large African land mammal' and 'There is just one problem with Edward: he never listens.'

comma

The comma (,) has a number of uses. We use commas to separate the items in a list of more than two things: for example, 'I like melon, grapes, banana, raspberries, strawberries and ice cream.'

We also use a comma in a sentence that includes direct speech. The comma indicates a pause between the spoken words and the rest of the sentence: for example, '"I'm hungry," complained Matt' or 'Jane said, "I've read that book."'

A pair of commas can also be used to separate a weak interruption from the rest of the sentence: for example, 'Isabella, who is my youngest sister, has black hair.'

comma splice

A comma splice occurs when two independent clauses are linked by a comma (rather than a coordinating conjunction, colon or semicolon): for example, 'John hates coffee, he drinks tea instead.' This is usually considered to be an error.

command

A command is a type of sentence used to give instructions. Most often, a command is given using an imperative sentence: for example, 'Get out!' or 'Hurry up!'

A command can also be given using other sentence types: for example, 'You must leave', which is a declarative sentence.

common noun

A noun denotes a person, place or thing. Every noun that is not the given name or title of a specific person, place or thing is a common noun. For example, the generic words 'dog', 'child', 'day' and 'country' are all common nouns. Each of these words can be used to denote any member of its class. In contrast, the names 'Rover', 'Harriet', 'Saturday' and 'Wales' refer to specific people, places and things; these words are proper nouns. Common nouns can be collective (or not), countable or uncountable, abstract or concrete.

comparative adjective

A comparative adjective describes a noun or a pronoun by comparing it with one or more other items. For example, in the sentence 'Fred is **younger** than Jim and Ted', the comparative adjective 'younger' describes 'Fred' by comparing him with 'Jim and Ted'.

Comparatives can be formed by adding the suffix ‹-er› to the positive adjective (as in 'young**er**' or 'long**er**'), or by using the word 'more' before the positive adjective (as in '**more** difficult' or '**more** careful').

complement

A complement is a word or phrase that provides more information about something. There are a number of different types of complement.

A subject complement is a word or phrase that follows a linking verb, and either describes the subject or denotes something equivalent to the subject. For example, in the sentence 'My cat is black', the word 'black' is the complement of – and describes – the subject 'my cat'. Similarly, in the sentence 'This woman is my aunt', 'my aunt' is the complement of the subject 'this woman'.

An object complement is a word or phrase that follows the object of a sentence, and either describes it or denotes something equivalent to it. For example, in the sentence 'Arthur made Kate very unhappy', 'very unhappy' is the complement of the object 'Kate'.

Complements can also 'complete' other parts of a sentence. For example, in the sentence 'Scarlet is scared of the dark', 'of the dark' is the complement of the adjective 'scared'.

complement clause

A complement clause is a type of subordinate clause that follows and completes a verb, a noun or an adjective. For example, in the sentence 'She knows that I cannot come', the complement clause 'that I cannot come' completes the verb 'knows'. Similarly, in the sentence 'The skirt that you are wearing has a hole in it', the complement clause 'that you are wearing' completes and describes the noun 'skirt'. Finally, in the sentence 'I am certain that the Earth is a sphere', the complement clause 'that the Earth is a sphere' completes the adjective 'certain'.

complex sentence

A complex sentence is a sentence that contains a main clause and at least one subordinate clause. For example, the sentence 'I drink lots of water because it is good for me' is complex because it contains a main clause ('I drink lots of water') and a subordinate clause ('because it is good for me').

compound sentence

A compound sentence is a sentence that contains two or more main clauses, but no subordinate clauses. The main clauses are usually joined together with a coordinating conjunction ('for', 'and', 'nor', 'but', 'or', 'yet' or 'so'), but can also be joined with a semicolon. The sentence 'Jane likes toast but Jonny hates it' is compound because it contains two main clauses ('Jane likes toast' and 'Jonny hates it'), which are joined together by the coordinating conjunction 'but'.

compound-complex sentence

A compound-complex sentence is a sentence that contains at least two main clauses and at least one subordinate clause. For example, 'While I looked for some new shoes, I saw this lovely dress and I bought it.' This sentence has two main clauses: 'I saw this lovely dress' and 'I bought it', which are joined by the coordinating conjunction 'and', and one subordinate clause, 'While I looked for some new shoes', which is introduced by the subordinating conjunction 'while'.

compound word

A compound word is a long word formed by the combination of two or more root words: for example, 'blackbird', 'toothbrush', 'starfish', 'nevertheless' and 'butterfly'. Compounding is very common in English.

In a compound word, the first component word is usually modifying the second component word; so a 'blackbird' is a type of bird that is black. However, it is not always possible to understand a compound word through its component words:

a 'starfish' is not really a fish, and the origin of the word 'butterfly' is even less clear.

comprehension

To 'comprehend' means to grasp or understand. In order to read a piece of text, a child simply has to decode the written words and produce the spoken words, but to comprehend a piece of text they must also be able to derive meaning from those words.

concrete noun

A concrete noun is a word that denotes a thing that can be experienced with one or more of the five senses, something that exists in a physical form. The words 'desk', 'feather', 'shirt' and 'cat' are all concrete nouns.

conditional

The conditional mood is used when talking about something that might be the case (or might *have been* the case) under certain circumstances. Conditional sentences are usually of the form 'if [...] then [...]': for example, 'If I had been there then I would have helped.' The conditional mood is a type of **irrealis** mood.

conjugation

The grammatical person, as well as the aspect and tense, affects the form of the verb we use in a sentence. For example, we say 'I am', but 'you are' and 'she is'. 'Am', 'are' and 'is' are all parts of the verb 'to be', together with 'was' and 'were' (which denote the past tense), and 'been' and 'being' (which are participles).

In the Jolly Phonics grammar programme, children are encouraged to practise verb conjugations regularly by saying the pronouns in order and using the correct form of the verb after each one.

conjunction

A conjunction (also known as a 'connective') is a word that is used to join parts of a sentence together. Conjunctions can be 'coordinating', 'subordinating' or 'correlative'. A coordinating conjunction (such as 'for', 'and', 'nor', 'but', 'or', 'yet' or 'so') joins together two main clauses, while a subordinating conjunction (such as 'because', 'if', 'while' and many others) introduces a subordinate clause. Correlative conjunctions always come in pairs (such as 'not only [...] but also', 'both [...] and'). They connect equal pairs of words, phrases or clauses within a sentence.

See also coordinating conjunction, correlative conjunction and subordinating conjunction.

connective

(see conjunction)

consonant

A consonant is any sound that is not a vowel. For example, /ch/, /h/ and /t/ are all consonants, but /a/, /ee/ and /ou/ are not.

Technically, a consonant sound is made when the lips, throat, teeth or tongue partially, or completely, prevent the air from flowing through the vocal tract. For example, the /ck/ sound is produced when the back of the tongue cuts off the flow of air. In contrast, a vowel sound is made with an open vocal tract.

consonant blend

A consonant blend is when two or more consonants appear together in a word with no vowels in between: for example, the ‹str-› in 'stripe'.

continuous (verbs)

The continuous (also known as the 'progressive') is a verb form that denotes an action that continues over a period of time. The continuous is formed by adding the present participle to the auxiliary verb 'to be': for example, 'I **am running**'; 'They **are running**'; 'You **were running**'.

contraction

Sometimes, we shorten a pair of words and join them together to form a contraction. We use an apostrophe to show where the missing letter(s) used to be: for example, 'isn't' ('is not'), 'they'll' ('they will') and 'haven't' ('have not'). We can also shorten single words in this way, such as 'can't' (cannot). Contractions are informal and should only be written when quoting speech, or in a friendly note.

coordinating conjunction

A conjunction (also known as a 'connective') is a word that is used to join parts of a sentence together. A coordinating conjunction joins together two main clauses to form a compound sentence (or a compound-complex sentence). The words 'for', 'and', 'nor', 'but', 'or', 'yet' and 'so' are the coordinating conjunctions, and can be remembered with the acronym FANBOYS.

coordination

Coordination describes an equal relationship between clauses, phrases or words. A coordinated pair of clauses, phrases or words is joined by a coordinating conjunction ('for', 'and', 'nor', 'but', 'or', 'yet', 'so').

For example, in the compound sentence 'Jane likes toast but Jonny hates it', both of the clauses ('Jane likes toast' and 'Jonny hates it') are main clauses, meaning each could form a complete sentence by itself, so they are joined as an equal pair by the coordinating conjunction 'but'.

Similarly, in the sentence 'Freddie likes football and tennis', the two nouns, 'football' and 'tennis', are joined by the coordinating conjunction 'and' because, as an equal pair, they are the object of the verb 'likes'.

copulative verb

(see linking verb)

correlative conjunction

Correlative conjunctions always come in pairs. They connect equal pairs of words, phrases or clauses within a sentence. For example, in the sentence 'We can have either tea or coffee' the correlative conjunctions 'either [...] or' connect the two nouns 'tea' and 'coffee'. Other correlative conjunction pairs include the following: 'not only [...] but also', 'both [...] and', 'neither [...] nor', 'just as [...] so' and 'no sooner [...] than'.

count noun

(see countable noun)

countable noun

Countable nouns (also known as 'count' nouns) are discrete items that can be counted. Countable nouns can be singular or plural, and can be modified by a numeral. 'Cat', for example, is a count noun. We say 'cat' for the singular and 'cat**s**' for the plural. We can also use a numeral to specify a particular number of cats, such as '**twelve** cats'. Other countable nouns include 'tree', 'child', 'table', 'bird' and 'car', but there are many more.

When talking about a smaller number of countable nouns we usually use the word 'fewer', as in '**fewer** cats' or '**fewer** tables' In contrast, when talking about a smaller amount of an uncountable noun we usually use the word 'less', as in '**less** water'.

D

dash

A pair of dashes can be used to separate an interruption from the rest of the sentence, as in the sentence: 'My brother – a really nice guy – is an astrophysicist'. When the interruption comes at the end of the sentence only one dash is used: for example, 'I recently took up parkour – another word for "freerunning"'.

declarative

A declarative is one of the four sentence types (the other three being interrogative, imperative and exclamatory). A declarative sentence is usually used to make a statement: for example, 'The children are happy' or 'I have read that book.'

declension

Most nouns have different forms for singular and plural. This inflection is called 'declension'. The singular noun form is usually the same as the root form of the word, as in 'mug' and 'fox'. The plural form is usually made by adding ‹-s› or ‹-es› to the end of the noun, as in 'mug**s**' and 'fox**es**'. However, some nouns, such as 'mouse' and 'woman', have irregular plurals, which are formed by modifying the root word or adding an unusual ending, as in 'mice' and 'women'.

definite article

The word 'the' is the definite article. It can be used before singular or plural nouns: for example, '**the** dog' or '**the** boys'.

definition

A definition explains the meaning of a word. Word definitions can be found in a dictionary.

demonstrative

Demonstratives are words such as 'this', 'that', 'these' and 'those', which help to indicate which particular person or thing the speaker is talking about.

Demonstratives can function as adjectives (as in 'Pass me **those** shoes') or pronouns (as in 'Pass me **those**'). Demonstrative adjectives are sometimes referred to as 'demonstrative determiners'.

dependent clause

(see subordinate clause)

determiner

A determiner is usually understood to be a special type of adjective. However, some grammarians choose to classify determiners as a distinct part of speech.

A determiner specifies which particular noun the speaker is referring to. It is usually the first word in a noun phrase: for example, in the noun phrase 'this brown rabbit', the first word, 'this', is the determiner. Other determiners include the words 'a', 'the', 'these', 'that', 'many', 'all'

and 'both'.

dialect

Dialect refers to the variety of language, including vocabulary and grammar, used by a particular person or by a particular group of people.

Dialects are typically classed as 'standard' or 'non-standard'. For example, 'I **done** my homework' would be classed as non-standard English, while 'I **have done** my homework' (or 'I **did** my homework') would be classed as Standard English. Standard English is the dialect that has been established as the universal norm and, as such, it is the dialect used for formal spoken and written communication.

Dialect is distinct from accent, which refers to the way in which the words of a language are pronounced by a particular person or a particular group of people.

digraph

A digraph is a pair of letters that represents a single speech sound, or phoneme. For example, the digraph ‹ai› in the word 'rain' is written with two letters, but makes one sound: /ai/.

direct object

In a sentence, the direct object is the noun or pronoun that 'receives' the verb action. For example, the object of the sentence 'Jack bought pasta' is 'pasta': this is the thing that is bought.

direct speech

Direct speech is the spoken words of a person. When we quote direct speech in writing, we use opening speech marks immediately before the spoken words and closing speech marks afterwards. It is important to quote the spoken words exactly as they were said: for example, '"I'm tired," said Tim.'

Direct speech should not be confused with indirect speech (or reported speech), which does not involve quoting exact words: for example, 'Tim said that he was tired.'

E

ellipsis

Ellipsis means omission. Sometimes, when speaking or writing, we leave out words or phrases that are expected and do not need to be said. For example, in the sentence 'Bill can ride a bike and Joe can ride a bike, too' we can leave out the crossed out words and the sentence still makes sense.

When we want to omit words from a direct quotation, or leave a sentence or thought unfinished, we indicate where words have been missed out by inserting a string of three dots within a pair of square brackets, as in the sentence 'According to the most recent data, "young children [...] learn better in a secure environment."' This string of dots is also referred to as ellipsis.

embedded question

Occasionally, a question is not asked directly, but instead forms part of a longer sentence. This type of question is known as an 'embedded' or 'indirect' question. For example, inside the statement 'I don't know where the dictionaries are' there is, albeit with a different word order, the embedded question 'Where are the dictionaries?' The same embedded question can be found inside the direct question 'Can you tell me where the dictionaries are?' An embedded question is a type of subordinate clause.

etymology

The history of a word (its origin and the evolution of its meaning and form) is called its etymology. For example, the English word 'yacht' (a small sailing boat) comes originally from the Middle Low German word 'jachtschip' (meaning 'ship for chasing or hunting') via the Dutch word 'jaght' (meaning 'hunt'). Over the years, the meaning and spelling of this word have gradually changed, giving us the form of the word we use today.

The English language has acquired many of its words in this way, using words and morphemes from other languages (particularly Latin, Greek and French). Indeed, some modern English words contain morphemes from two different languages: for example, the word 'television' stems from the Greek word 'tele' (meaning 'far') and the

Latin word 'visio' (meaning 'seeing'). These words are called hybrid words.

exclamation

An exclamation is a phrase or sentence that shows strong emotion. Often, an exclamation is made with an exclamatory sentence: for example, 'What a great book!'

Exclamations can also be single words or incomplete sentences: for example, 'Ow!' or 'Oh, no!' We use an exclamation mark (!) at the end of an exclamation.

exclamation mark

An exclamation mark (!) is used at the end of an exclamation to indicate that the writer or speaker feels strongly about something.

exclamatory

An exclamatory (also known as an exclamative) is one of the four sentence types (the other three being interrogative, imperative and declarative). An exclamatory sentence is usually used for an exclamation: for example, 'Oh dear!' or 'What a cool song this is!'

F

filler

A filler is a sound, word or phrase, such as 'um', 'well...' or 'er', that is uttered during a pause in conversation. The speaker uses the filler to indicate that he or she has not yet finished speaking, but has instead paused momentarily to think.

finite (verbs)

Verb forms that are inflected for subject and tense are said to be finite. In contrast, the infinitive (the 'to-' form of the verb) has no inflection. For example, in the sentence 'Mary runs regularly', the verb 'runs' is finite; it has been inflected for the third person singular ('Mary') and the simple present tense.

Every complete main clause must have a finite verb. Non-finite verbs, such as participles and infinitives, cannot be the only verb in a clause and can only be used with a finite verb. Therefore, in the sentence 'It **took** courage **to continue**', the verb 'took' is an example of a finite verb, whereas 'to continue' is non-finite because it is in the infinitive.

first person

In English, as in most languages, we have different personal pronouns for each of the different grammatical persons. The personal pronouns for the first person singular are 'I' and 'me', and for the first person plural they are 'we' and 'us'.

The first person singular always denotes the speaker (or writer). Using the first person plural means that the speaker (or writer) is communicating on behalf of a group to which they belong.

fronted adverbial

(see fronting)

fronting

Fronting refers to the placement of a word or phrase that would normally be positioned elsewhere in a sentence at the beginning of the sentence. For example, in the sentence 'On the roof, there was a little cat' the prepositional phrase 'on the roof', which would usually come at the end of the sentence (as in 'There was a little cat on the roof'), has been placed at the beginning of the sentence. Adverbials, such as 'on the roof', are often fronted in this way.

full stop

A full stop (.) is used at the end of a sentence that communicates a statement: for example, 'Those are my socks.' A full stop is sometimes called a 'period'.

future (verbs)

Technically, there is no future tense in English; instead, we typically indicate the future by using an auxiliary verb ('shall' or 'will') together with the main verb: for example, 'I **shall go** swimming'; 'you **will be having** supper'; or 'she **will have walked** to work.'

The future can also be formed with the verb 'to be', the word 'going' and the infinitive form of the verb: for example, 'He **is going to read** the newspaper.'

G

gerund

A gerund is a verb form ending in ‹-ing›, which functions as a noun. Alone, or as part of a noun phrase, a gerund can be used as the subject of a sentence (as in '**cycling** is an excellent pastime'), the object of a sentence (as in 'I loathe **drinking** coffee'), or the object of a preposition (as in 'My headache was brought on by his **shouting**').

grammar

Grammar refers to the study of word structure (morphology) and sentence structure (syntax).

grammatical agreement

In English, as in most languages, certain words in a sentence have to 'agree with', or correspond to, other words in that sentence. In English, grammatical agreement is concerned with grammatical person, number and, occasionally, gender.

A verb is inflected (changes form) so as to agree with the grammatical person that is acting as the subject of that verb. For example, we would say 'I **like** flowers' (first person singular), but 'She **likes** flowers' (third person singular). In the second sentence, the third person singular marker (‹-s›) has been added to the verb 'like' so that it agrees with the third person singular subject 'she'.

Whether the subject is singular or plural (grammatical number) can also affect the verb form. So, we say 'The rabbit **eats** carrots' in the singular, but 'The rabbit**s eat** carrots' in the plural.

Similarly, the articles must agree with the noun they describe. The indefinite articles 'a' and 'an' can only be used with singular nouns, but the definite article 'the' can be used with either singular or plural nouns.

The personal pronouns, possessive pronouns and possessive adjectives are affected by gender. So we use the words 'he', 'him' and 'his' for the masculine, 'she', 'her' and 'hers' for the feminine, 'they', 'them' and 'theirs' for the non-gender specific and 'it' and 'its' for the neuter.

grammatical person

The grammatical person is closely related to personal pronouns. The first person singular ('I', 'me') is used when the speaker is referring to him, her or themself; the second person singular ('you', 'you') is used when the speaker is referring to the addressee; the third person singular ('he', 'she', 'they', 'him', 'her', 'them', 'it') is used to refer to someone else; first person plural ('we', 'us') is used when the speaker is referring to a group to which they also belong; the second person plural ('you', 'you') is used when the speaker is referring to more than one addressee; the third person plural ('they', 'them') is used to refer to more than one other person.

grapheme

A grapheme is the smallest unit of written language. A grapheme could be a letter, a numeral or a punctuation mark.

grapheme-phoneme correspondence

In written English, each letter or digraph represents a spoken sound. The relationship between a letter (or digraph) and the sound it represents is sometimes referred to as a 'grapheme-phoneme correspondence'. In Jolly Phonics materials, we use the term 'letter sound' to refer to this correspondence.

H

head

Most phrases have a 'head' word, which governs the function of the phrase. So, a noun phrase, such as 'the big wooden bowl', has a noun, 'bowl' in this case, as its head. Similarly, a verb phrase has a verb as its head; an adjective phrase has an adjective as its head; an adverb phrase has an adverb as its head; and a prepositional phrase has a preposition as its head.

heterograph

The word 'heterograph' comes from Greek and means 'different write' (or 'different spelling'). Heterographs are words that have different spellings and meanings, but sound the same: for example, 'there', 'their' and 'they're'.

heteronym

The word 'heteronym' comes from Greek and means 'different name' (or 'different pronunciation'). Heteronyms are words that have different pronunciations and meanings, but identical spellings. For example, 'row' could mean 'argument' (as in 'We had a **row**'), or 'paddle with oars' (as in 'They **row** to the island'). A heteronym is a type of homograph.

homograph

The word 'homograph' comes from Greek and means 'same write' (or 'same spelling'). Homographs are words that have identical spellings but different meanings.

Some homographs have different pronunciations; these homographs are also heteronyms. For example, 'minute' could refer to a certain amount of time (as in 'I'll be there in a **minute**'), or it could describe something very small (as in 'That mouse is **minute**').

Other homographs have the same pronunciation; these homographs are called homonyms. For example, 'bat' could refer to an animal (as in 'The **bat** lives in a cave'), or a piece of sports equipment (as in 'He hit the ball with a **bat**').

homonym

The word 'homonym' comes from Greek and means 'same name' (or 'same pronunciation'). Homonyms are words that have the same pronunciation and spelling, but different meanings. For example, 'left' could mean 'went out' (as in 'He **left** the house'), or it could mean the opposite of 'right' (as in 'They turned **left**'). A homonym is a type of homograph.

homophone

The word 'homophone' comes from Greek and means 'same sound'. Homophones are words that sound the same but have different meanings.

Some homophones have different spellings. These homophones are also heterographs: for example, 'to', 'two' and 'too'.

Other homophones have identical spellings; these homophones are also homographs and homonyms. For example, 'rose' could refer to a flower (as in 'There is a **rose** in my garden'), or it could be the past tense to the verb 'to rise' (as in 'The sun **rose** over the horizon').

hop-over ‹e›

(see split digraph)

hybrid word

A hybrid word contains morphemes from two different languages: for example, the word 'television' stems from the Greek word 'tele' (meaning 'far') and the Latin word 'visio' (meaning 'seeing').

hyphen

A hyphen (-) is used between words that are linked closely together, so as to avoid ambiguity. For example, the phrase 'eight year old children' is ambiguous; it could refer to eight children who are all one year old, or to an unspecified number of children who are all eight years old. With hyphens we can make our meaning clear: 'eight year-old children' refers to eight children who are all one year old, while 'eight-year-old children' refers to an unspecified number of children who are all eight years old. We also use hyphens when writing the numbers 21 to 99 as words (as in 'twenty-one' and 'ninety-nine'), and when the first part of a compound word is a single letter (as in 'X-ray' and 'T-shirt').

I

idiom

An idiom is a phrase or a fixed expression whose meaning cannot be worked out from the meanings of its component words. For example, the idiomatic English phrase 'to let the cat out of the bag' means 'to divulge a secret'. The phrase's figurative meaning is very different from its literal meaning.

imperative

An imperative is one of the four sentence types (the other three being interrogative, exclamatory and declarative). Imperative sentences often have an implied, rather than overtly stated, subject (which is usually taken to be 'you'), and they use the bare infinitive verb form (the infinitive form of the verb, without the word 'to'). An imperative sentence is usually used in a command: for example, 'Come here'; 'Give me that'; 'Don't shout'. Imperative sentences can also be used to give warnings ('Beware of the bull!'), instructions ('Add a pinch of salt'), advice ('Read the instructions first'), suggestions ('Taste this ice cream'), invitations ('Come back anytime') and requests ('Please close the door').

The imperative mood is the grammatical mood used in imperative sentences. It is a type of irrealis mood.

indefinite articles

The indefinite articles are the words 'a' and 'an'. All articles are determiners, which are themselves special types of adjectives. 'A' is used before singular nouns beginning with a consonant sound (as in 'a man' or 'a dog'), and 'an' is used before singular nouns beginning with a vowel sound (as in 'an octopus' or 'an eel').

independent clause

(see main clause)

indicative

The indicative mood is used for statements of fact: for example, 'This book is green' or 'We live in England'. The indicative mood is a type of realis mood.

indirect object

The indirect object is the noun or pronoun that is affected by the verb action, but is not its direct object. For example, in the sentence 'John gave Annabelle flowers', the direct object is 'flowers' (the flowers are what is being given), but there is also an indirect object: 'Annabelle'. 'Annabelle' is not being given in the sentence, but she is indirectly affected by the action because she is the person to whom the flowers are given.

indirect speech

Indirect speech tells you what someone has said without using their exact words, as opposed to direct speech, which involves quoting exact words. 'I asked her how she had been', 'She complained about the weather' and 'They spoke words of love' are all examples of indirect speech.

infinitive (verbs)

The infinitive form of the verb is the uninflected form (with or without the word 'to'): for example, 'to run', 'run', 'to play', 'play', 'to see', 'see'. When the infinitive form of the verb is used without the word 'to' in front of it, it is known as the 'bare' infinitive.

inflection

Some words, particularly verbs, change for grammatical reasons.

This change of form is called 'inflection'. The verb 'to be', for example, has many inflected forms, including 'am', 'is', 'are', 'being', 'was', 'were' and 'been'. When verbs are inflected it is called 'conjugation'.

Nouns can also have inflected forms: for example, 'child' becomes 'children' in the plural, and 'cat' becomes 'cats'. When nouns are inflected it is called 'declension'.

interjection

An interjection is a phrase, a word or a filler (such as 'um' or 'er'), which conveys emotion, but does not constitute a complete sentence. Many interjections are also exclamations: for example, 'Goodness me!' and 'Wow!'

interrogative

An interrogative is one of the four sentence types (the other three being imperative, exclamatory and declarative. An interrogative sentence is used to ask a question: for example, 'Do you like lemonade?' or 'Where is the car?'

A declarative sentence can be turned into an interrogative sentence by moving the auxiliary verb (or the verb 'to be') to the front of the sentence. So, 'We **shall** go to the park' becomes '**Shall** we go to the park?' and 'This **is** the way to the park' becomes '**Is** this the way to the park?' Where there is no auxiliary verb, the verb 'to do' is added at the beginning of a sentence to form the interrogative: for example, 'You like tea' becomes '**Do** you like tea?'

intransitive verb

An intransitive verb is a verb that does not take a direct object. Some verbs never take an object and are always intransitive: for example, the verb 'to sleep', as in the sentence 'I sleep soundly.' Other verbs can be intransitive or transitive depending on the context: for example, in the sentence 'The door opens', the verb 'to open' is intransitive; however, in the sentence 'She opens her present', the verb 'to open' is transitive, taking 'present' as its direct object.

See also transitive verb.

inverted commas

(see speech marks)

irrealis moods

Irrealis moods are the grammatical moods used when talking about wishes, suggestions, desires, demands, possibilities or hypotheses: in other words, anything that is not actually known to be the case. For example, in the sentence 'I suggest that John stay for lunch', John's staying for lunch is not a fact, but a suggestion; it might or might not happen. This sentence is in the **subjunctive mood**, which is a type of irrealis mood. Other types of irrealis mood include the **conditional** and the **imperative**.

irregular

An irregular word is a word that does not follow the expected pattern. For example, the verb 'to be' is very irregular: 'I **am**, you **are**, he/she/it **is**' and so on. In contrast, the verb 'to walk' is very regular: 'I **walk**, you **walk**, he/she/it **walks**'.

J K L

letter

A letter is a type of grapheme that is used to denote a sound in speech.

letter sound

The term 'letter sound' is used in Jolly Phonics materials to refer to the sound made by a letter or by a letter combination.

A letter sound can often be equated to a phoneme. For example, the sound made by the letter ‹a› in 'cat' is a single phoneme. Similarly, the single sound made by the letter combination ‹sh›, as in 'sheep', is one phoneme. However, the sound made by some single letters, such as ‹x›, is composed of two phonemes, in this case /k/ and /s/. So, /x/ is one letter sound, but corresponds to two phonemes.

In Jolly Phonics materials, letter sounds are commonly written between two slash marks, like this: /ai/.

lexical verb

A lexical verb is a main verb. For example, in the sentence 'We have run,' the lexical verb is 'run', while 'have' is the auxiliary verb. Lexical verbs can be used with or without an auxiliary verb.

linguistics

Linguistics is the study of language and language structure. It is particularly concerned with the way in which utterances convey meaning. Branches of linguistics include phonology, morphology, syntax and semantics.

linking verb

A linking verb (also known as a 'copulative' verb) links the subject of a sentence to its complement. The most common linking verb is the verb 'to be', as in the sentence 'A sheep **is** a mammal.' Other linking verbs include 'to seem' (as in 'She **seems** nice'), 'to feel' (as in 'I **feel** sick'), and 'to become' (as in 'The sea **became** calm').

long vowel

The long vowel sounds are /ai/ (as in 'train'), /ee/ (as in 'tree'), /ie/ (as in 'cried'), /oa/ (as in 'toad'), and /ue/ (as in 'cue'). These are also the names of the five vowel letters: ‹A›, ‹E›, ‹I›, ‹O› and ‹U›.

M

magic ‹e›
(see split digraph)

main clause

A clause is a group of words that contains a verb and a subject and makes sense. A main (or 'independent') clause can stand alone as a sentence. For example, the main clause 'I bought some shoes' works as a complete sentence by itself. Every complete sentence contains at least one main clause.

mass noun
(see uncountable noun)

modal auxiliary verb

A modal auxiliary verb (or 'modal verb') is a special kind of auxiliary verb. Modal auxiliaries are used to indicate modality: probability or improbability, certainty or possibility, ability, obligation or permission. For example, the modal auxiliary verb 'might' in the sentence 'I **might** go to the theatre' indicates possibility, while the modal auxiliary 'should' in the sentence 'You **should** be quiet' indicates obligation. Other modal auxiliary verbs include 'can', 'could', 'may', 'must', 'shall', 'will' and 'would'.

Like other auxiliary verbs, modal auxiliaries can be negated: for example, 'They **couldn't** swim' or 'They **could not** swim.' Unlike other verbs, a modal auxiliary verb only exists in a single, finite form, and this form does not change according to tense or subject. For example, we say 'He must come to the party' rather than 'He must**s** come to the party.'

modal verb

(see modal auxiliary verb)

mode

(see mood)

modifier

A modifier is a word or phrase that restricts ('modifies') the meaning of another word or phrase, making it more specific. For example, the noun phrase 'the cat' could refer to any cat, but when the modifiers 'young', 'ginger', 'tabby' and 'who lives next door' are added, the resulting phrase, 'the young, ginger, tabby cat who lives next door', has a much more precise meaning.

monosyllabic

A monosyllabic word has only one syllable. For example, the words 'run', 'jump', 'cat' and 'through' are all monosyllabic, while 'idea', 'table' and 'scooter' contain multiple syllables and are therefore known as polysyllabic words.

mood

Grammatical mood (or mode) is concerned with the actuality or reality of what a speaker is saying. Grammatical moods fall into two categories: realis moods, which are used for statements of fact, and irrealis moods which are used when talking about wishes, suggestions, desires, demands, possibilities or hypotheses: in other words, anything that is not a statement of fact.

morpheme

A morpheme is the smallest linguistic unit that has meaning. Some words, such as 'kind', consist of a single morpheme, but other words contain more than one morpheme. 'Unkindness', for example, has three morphemes: 'un-', 'kind' and '-ness'. All three of these morphemes contribute to the meaning of the whole word, but only the root word, 'kind', can stand alone.

Unlike words, not all morphemes can stand alone and convey a meaning. The prefix 'un-' when uttered in isolation has no meaning; it is only when it is combined with the root word 'kind' to make 'unkind' that it conveys a meaning.

morphology

Morphology is the study of word structure. All words are made up of one or more morphemes. Every word has at least one root word, and it may also have prefixes, suffixes and inflections. For example, the plural noun 'toothbrushes' has three morphemes: the two root words 'tooth' and 'brush', and the plural inflection '-es'. Morphology is a branch of linguistics.

N

non-count noun

(see uncountable noun)

noun

A noun denotes a person, place or thing. On the most basic level, nouns can be divided into proper nouns (such as 'Abdul', 'Mr Smith', 'Dublin' and 'December') and common nouns (such as 'child', 'man', 'city' and 'month').

noun phrase

A noun phrase (often abbreviated to 'NP') is any phrase that has a noun as its head word: for example, 'the fluffy, young **lamb**' or 'this enormous **piece** of chocolate cake'.

object

In a sentence, the direct object is the noun or pronoun that 'receives' the verb action. For example, the object of the sentence 'Jack bought pasta' is 'pasta': this is the thing that is bought. A sentence can also have an indirect object. The indirect object is the noun or pronoun that is affected by the verb action, but is not its direct object. For example, in the sentence 'John gave Annabelle flowers', the direct object is 'flowers' (the flowers are what is being given), but there is also an indirect object: 'Annabelle'. 'Annabelle' is not being given in the sentence, but she is indirectly affected by the action because she is the person to whom the flowers are given. A noun or pronoun can also be the object of a preposition (or the 'oblique' object), as in the sentence 'Stand next to **them**.'

Although a sentence must have a subject to be complete, it does not necessarily need to have an object. If a sentence has an intransitive verb (which does not take a direct object), it is complete without an object. For example, 'I walk quickly' is a complete sentence even though there is no object.

object of a preposition

The noun, noun phrase or pronoun that follows a preposition is the object of that preposition (or the 'oblique' object). For example, in the sentence 'Play with Fred', 'Fred' is the object of the preposition 'with'.

object pronoun

Pronouns are the little words used to replace nouns. The object pronouns are as follows: 'me', 'you', 'him', 'her', 'it', 'us', 'you' and 'them'. These pronouns are used as the object (direct, indirect or oblique object) of a sentence: for example, 'The dog likes **me**'; 'Give the book to **her**'; 'Sit by **him**.'

oblique object

(see object of a preposition)

onomatopoeia

Onomatopoeia is the term for words that sound like the things they denote. The words for machinery sounds and animal noises, such as 'beep', 'clang', 'zoom', 'moo', 'purr' and 'ribbit', are almost always onomatopoeic. Other common onomatopoeic words include 'hiccup', 'boing' and 'zap'.

P

paragraph

Paragraphs consist of one or more sentences placed together. They are used to organise information in a piece of writing. Each paragraph starts on a new line, which is usually indented, and is made up of sentences that describe one idea or topic.

parentheses

Parentheses, also known as round brackets, look like this: (). A pair of parentheses is used to separate an interruption from the rest of the sentence. The interruption could provide additional information, as in the sentence: 'My brother (who is six years older than me) is an astrophysicist', or it could explain or define a term that has just been used: for example, 'I recently took up parkour (another word for 'freerunning').'

parsing

Parsing is the name given to the exercise of identifying the function of words in a sentence. Each word must be looked at in context to decide which part of speech it is, as many words can function as more than one part of speech: for exam-ple, the word 'light' can be a noun ('a light'), a verb ('to light'), or an adjective ('a light blue').

particle

Particles are words (typically short words) that must be linked to another word to convey meaning. For example, the non-verb parts of a phrasal verb, such as the 'in' of 'give in', are particles, as is the word 'to' when it forms part of an infinitive verb, such as 'to run'.

part of speech

Words are divided into different categories according to their function. These categories are called 'parts of speech' (or, sometimes, 'word classes'). The words in the English language can be divided into the following categories: nouns, pronouns, verbs, adjectives, adverbs, conjunctions, prepositions, interjections and determiners. (Although determiners are sometimes counted as a type of adjective.)

passive voice

The passive voice is used when the noun, pronoun or noun phrase that 'receives' the action of the verb (which would normally make it the object of that verb) appears as the subject of the verb. The noun, pronoun or noun phrase that 'does' the verb action (and would normally be the subject) either forms part of a prepositional phrase introduced by the word 'by', or is removed from the sentence altogether. For example, the sentence 'The hamster bit the boy', which is in the more usual active voice, could be rewritten in the passive voice as 'The boy was bitten by the hamster', or even just 'The boy was bitten'. In both of these latter sentences, the boy is on the receiving end of the verb action (the biting), but he appears as the subject of the sentence.

The passive voice is formed with the auxiliary verb 'to be' (or 'to get') and the past participle of the main verb, as in the sentences 'This book **was written** by Iris Murdoch' and 'Our postman **got knocked** off his bike.'

past participle (verbs)

The past participle is usually formed by adding ‹-ed› to the verb root, as in 'look**ed**', 'walk**ed**' and 'wait**ed**'. However, some irregular verbs take ‹-en› instead, as in 'tak**en**', 'brok**en**' and 'writt**en**'. In other irregular verbs, the verb root changes, as in 'swum', 'run' and 'sung'. Together with the auxiliary verb 'to have', the past participle forms the perfect tenses, as in the sentences 'You **had looked**'; 'She **has taken**'; and 'We **shall have swum**.' The past participle can also be used as an adjective, as in 'the **striped** shirt' and 'the **broken** chair'.

past tense (verbs)

The past tense is usually used when talking about something that has already taken place.

The simple past tense of regular verbs is formed by adding the suffix ‹-ed› to the verb root, as in the sentence 'We talk**ed** yesterday'.

The past continuous is formed with the past tense of the auxiliary verb 'to be' and the present participle, as in the sentence 'We **were** talk**ing** yesterday'.

The past perfect is formed with the past tense of the auxiliary verb 'to have' and the past participle, as in the sentence 'We **had** talk**ed** yesterday'.

Finally, the past perfect continuous is formed with the past tense of the auxiliary verb 'to have', the past participle of the verb 'to be' and the present participle, as in the sentence 'We **had been** talk**ing** yesterday.'

perfect (verbs)

The perfect is a verb form used for talking about the resulting state of an action that took place at an earlier time. The perfect is formed with the auxiliary verb 'to have' and the past participle: for example, 'I **have eaten**'; 'they **had eaten**'; 'she **has eaten**'.

perfect continuous (verbs)

The perfect continuous combines the perfect and continuous aspects. It is formed with the auxiliary verb 'to have', the past participle of the verb 'to be' and the present participle: for example, 'I **have been walking**'; 'They **had been walking**'; 'She **has been walking**'.

personal pronoun

Pronouns are used to replace nouns. There is a different personal pronoun for each grammatical person: 'I' is used for the first person singular; 'you' for the second person singular; 'he' (masculine), 'she' (feminine), 'they' (non-gender specific) or 'it' (neuter) for the third person singular; 'we' for the first person plural; 'you' for the second person plural; and 'they' for the third person plural.

Personal pronouns take different forms depending on whether they are the subject or object of the sentence. The subject pronouns are 'I', 'you', 'he', 'she', 'it', 'we', 'you' and 'they', and the object pronouns are 'me', 'you', 'him', 'her', 'it', 'us', 'you' and 'them'. So we say 'I like this cat', but 'this cat likes me'.

Although a variety of non-gender specific personal pronouns exist in current usage, non-gender specific language most commonly uses 'they' for the third person singular in the subjective case, 'them' for the third person singular in the objective case, 'their' for the possessive pronoun and 'themself' for the reflexive pronoun.

phoneme

A phoneme is a sound in speech. Phonemes are combined to make words. When writing, we represent each phoneme with one or more letters (also referred to as 'graphemes'). For example, the /sh/ sound in 'ship' is written with the letters ‹sh›. Occasionally, two different phonemes share the same spelling. For example, the words 'thigh' and 'thy' begin with the same digraph, ‹th›, but it represents a different phoneme in each word: 'thigh' begins with an unvoiced /th/ sound, while 'thy' begins with a voiced /th/ sound.

phonemic awareness

Phonemic awareness is the ability to recognise and manipulate individual sounds (phonemes). A typical phonemic awareness activity might involve identifying the individual sounds in a spoken word, or identifying pairs of words with the same initial sound. Phonemic awareness is part of phonological awareness.

phonics

(see synthetic phonics)

phonological awareness

Phonological awareness is the ability to recognise and manipulate both individual sounds (phonemes) and larger sound structures (such as syllables). Activities such as identifying pairs of rhyming words; splitting words into syllables; or identifying the individual sounds in a word all involve phonological awareness.

phonology

Phonology is the study of the system of phonemes in a language. It is particularly concerned with the way in which sounds are used to convey meaning. Phonology is a branch of linguistics.

phrasal verb

A phrasal verb consists of a verb and one or more other words (usually prepositions or adverbs). Together, these words make a new verb with a new meaning. For example, the verb 'to break' (meaning 'to fragment') can be combined with the preposition 'out' to make the phrasal verb 'to break out' meaning 'to escape'. The non-verb parts of a phrasal verb, such as the 'in' of 'give in', are called particles.

phrase

A phrase is a group of words that makes sense but does not form a complete main clause by itself. Most phrases have a head word, which governs the function of the phrase. So, a noun phrase, such as 'the big wooden bowl', has a noun, 'bowl' in this case, as its head. Similarly, a verb phrase has a verb as its head; an adjective phrase has an adjective as its head; an adverb phrase has an adverb as its head; and a prepositional phrase has a preposition as its head.

plural (nouns)

Most nouns change when they describe more than one of something. This inflection is called declension and the resulting word is called a plural.

The most common way to form a plural is by adding ‹-s› to the end of the noun, as in 'cat**s**', 'mug**s**' and 'face**s**', and by adding ‹-es› to those nouns which end in ‹sh›, ‹ch›, ‹s›, ‹z› or ‹x›, as in 'flash**es**', 'box**es**' and 'batch**es**'. Occasionally, the spelling of the word is altered slightly before adding ‹-es›, so 'kni**fe**' becomes 'kni**ves**' and 'fl**y**' becomes 'fl**ies**'. However, some nouns, such as 'mouse', 'woman' and 'child', have irregular plurals, which are formed by modifying the root word or adding an unusual ending, as in 'mice', 'women' and 'children'.

Some plurals, such as 'sheep', 'fish' and 'deer' have the same form for both singular and plural.

plural pronoun

The plural pronouns are used to denote more than one person. The first person plural ('we', or 'us' in the object position) is used when the speaker is referring to a group to which he or she also belongs; the second person plural ('you', 'you') is used when the speaker is referring to more than one addressee; the third person singular ('they', 'them') is used to refer to more than one other person.

polysyllabic

(see monosyllabic)

positive adjective

A positive adjective is the usual, basic form of an adjective. It describes a noun without comparing it to anything else. For example, the word 'tall', as in 'This girl is **tall**', is a positive adjective. In contrast, the comparative and superlative forms describe a noun by comparing it to something else, as in 'This girl is **taller** than the others' and 'This girl is the **tallest** in the class.'

possessive adjective

The possessive adjectives are 'my', 'your', 'his', 'her', 'its', 'our', 'your' and 'their'. These words correspond to the personal pronouns ('I', 'me', 'you', 'you', 'he', 'him', 'she', 'her', 'it', 'it', 'we', 'us', 'you', 'you', 'they', 'them'). A possessive adjective describes a noun by saying whose it is, so 'This is **my** book' means 'This is a book **belonging to me**.'

possessive noun

A possessive noun is formed by adding an apostrophe (') followed by the letter ‹s› to the end of a noun. A possessive noun acts as an adjective, describing the other noun by saying whose it is, as in '**Kofi's** book', '**Jane's** scarf' and 'the **cat's** basket'. When forming a possessive plural we omit the ‹s› after the apostrophe, so we get 'the boys' socks' and 'the trees' leaves' (rather than 'the boys**'s** socks' and 'the trees**'s** leaves'). However, if the plural is irregular and does not end in ‹s›, both the apostrophe and the ‹s› are added, as in 'the men**'s** watches' or the mice**'s** tails'.

possessive pronoun

The possessive pronouns are 'mine', 'yours', 'his', 'hers', 'its', 'ours', 'yours' and 'theirs'. These pronouns correspond to the personal pronouns and the possessive adjectives. A possessive pronoun replaces a noun and its possessive adjective, so that '**our** house' becomes '**ours**' and '**her** hat' becomes '**hers**'.

predicate

At its most basic level, a sentence has two parts: the subject (including any words that modify it) and the predicate (all other parts of the sentence, including the verb).

prefix

A prefix is a morpheme (usually one or more syllables) that is added to the beginning of a word to change its meaning. For example, when the prefix ‹un-› is added to the word 'happy', the resulting word, '**un**happy', means the opposite of the original word. Other common prefixes include ‹re-› (meaning 'again'), ‹non-› (meaning 'not'), ‹de-› (meaning 'undo' or 'remove'), and ‹semi-› (meaning 'half').

preposition

A preposition relates one noun or pronoun to another noun or pronoun in the sentence. Most prepositions, such as 'at', 'by', 'in', 'on' and 'under', indicate where something is or what it is moving towards, as in the sentence 'Maya is sitting **on** the sofa.'

However, not all prepositions indicate place; some prepositions relate a noun or pronoun to a time or event, as in the sentence 'The baby slept

through the night.' In this sentence, the words 'through the night' form a prepositional phrase, which acts as an adverb, modifying the verb 'slept'.

prepositional phrase

A prepositional phrase is made up from a preposition and its object (a noun or a pronoun). Prepositional phrases usually act as adverbs, describing where or when something happens, as in the sentence, 'The car sped **down the hill**.'

In certain contexts, however, prepositional phrases can act as adjectives. For example, in the sentence 'The book **about dinosaurs** is on the shelf', the prepositional phrase 'about dinosaurs' is acting as an adjective and describing the book.

present tense (verbs)

The present tense is normally used when talking about something that has not already taken place: usually something that is taking place now, or is relevant to the time of speaking.

The simple present tense is used for truths (such as 'Zebras **have** black and white stripes'), or for habitual actions or events (such as 'Ahmed **swims** every day'). The simple present form of the verb is usually the same as the verb root, as in 'I **talk**' and 'You **rush**'. However, if the subject is in the third person singular, the third person singular marker (‹-s› or ‹-es›) is added, as in 'He **talks**' and 'She **rushes**.'

The present continuous is formed with the present tense of the auxiliary verb 'to be' and the present participle, as in the sentence 'We **are talking**.'

The present perfect is formed with the present tense of the auxiliary verb 'to have' and the past participle, as in the sentence 'We **have** talk**ed**.'

Finally, the present perfect continuous is formed with the present tense of the auxiliary verb 'to have', the past participle of the verb 'to be' and the present participle, as in the sentence 'We **have been talking** for ages.'

present participle (verbs)

The present participle is formed by adding ‹-ing› to the verb root, as in 'looking', 'walking' and 'running'. Together with the auxiliary verb 'to be', the present participle forms the continuous tenses, as in the sentences 'You **were looking**'; 'She **is walking**'; and 'We **shall be running**.'

The present participle can also be used as an adjective, as in 'the **galloping** horse' and 'the **screaming** child'.

progressive

(see continuous)

pronoun

Pronouns are the little words used to replace nouns. They can help to make our writing more concise. For example, instead of saying 'John, Phoebe and Hamed walked to the park. John, Phoebe and Hamed played on the swings, and then John, Phoebe and Hamed went home', we can say 'John, Phoebe and Hamed walked to the park. **They** played on the swings, and then **they** went home.'

The personal pronouns take a different form when they are the subject of a sentence from that taken when they are the object of a sentence. The subject pronouns are 'I', 'you', 'he', 'she', 'it', 'we', 'you' and 'they', while the object pronouns are 'me', 'you', 'him', 'her', 'it', 'us', 'you' and 'them'. So we say '**I** like this cat', but 'this cat likes **me**'.

A possessive pronoun (such as 'mine', 'yours', 'his', 'hers', 'its', 'ours', 'yours' or 'theirs') is used to replace both a noun and its possessive adjective.

A reflexive pronoun (such as 'myself', 'yourself', 'himself', 'herself', 'themself', 'itself', 'ourselves', 'yourselves' or 'themselves' is used as the object of a verb when the subject and the object of that verb are the same person or thing.

See also personal pronoun, possessive pronoun, relative pronoun and reflexive pronoun.

proper noun
A proper noun is the particular given name of a person, a place, a building, a date or a thing: for example, 'Edward', 'Mrs Singh', 'the Tower of London', 'the Nile', 'Mount Everest', 'Japan', 'Europe', 'Monday', 'November' and 'New Year's Day'.

A proper noun always starts with a capital letter.

punctuation
Punctuation is the collective term for the marks that are used to give structure to text. The main punctuation marks used in the English language are as follows: the full stop (.), the comma (,), the question mark (**?**), the exclamation mark (!), speech marks (" "), the apostrophe ('), the colon (:), the semicolon (;), the hyphen (-), the dash (–), and parentheses ( ). Typically, features such as word spaces, paragraph breaks, capital letters, ellipses and bullet points are also considered to be punctuation.

question
A question is a sentence that is used to gain information. A question is asked using an interrogative sentence: for example, 'How did you do that?' or 'Can you swim?' We use a question mark (**?**) at the end of a question.

question mark
A question mark (**?**) is used at the end of an interrogative sentence to indicate that the writer or speaker is asking a question.

quotation marks
(see speech marks)

R

realis moods

Realis moods are used for making statements of fact: for example, 'Helen is a doctor', 'The cheetah ran faster than the rabbit', or 'This pen has run out'. All of these sentences are in the indicative mood, which is a type of realis mood.

Received Pronunciation

Received Pronunciation (often abbreviated to 'RP') is an accent used primarily in the South of England. Received Pronunciation is sometimes considered to be the accent of Standard English; however, it is perfectly possible to speak Standard English in an accent other than RP.

reflexive pronoun

A reflexive pronoun is used as the object of a verb when the subject and the object of that verb are the same person or thing. The reflexive pronouns correspond to the personal pronouns and are as follows: 'myself', 'yourself', 'himself', 'herself', 'themself', 'itself', 'ourselves', 'yourselves' and 'themselves'. A reflexive pronoun can be used as the direct object (as in 'He cut **himself** accidentally'), the indirect object (as in 'She bought **herself** a new dress'), or the object of a preposition (as in 'I am feeling very sorry for **myself**.')

register

When we write (or speak), we often vary our vocabulary, dialect and language style according to our situation or purpose. These variations of language are referred to as different registers. For example, a job application would have a very different register from an informal note.

regular

A regular word is a word that follows an expected pattern. For example, the verb 'to walk' is regular: 'I **walk**, you **walk**, he/she/it **walks**' and so on. In contrast, the verb 'to be' is very irregular: 'I **am**, you **are**, he/she/it **is**'.

relative adverb

A relative adverb is an adverb used to introduce a relative clause. For example, in the sentence 'I take my dog **wherever** I go', the relative adverb 'wherever' introduces the relative clause 'wherever I go'. Other relative adverbs include 'when', 'where' and 'why'.

relative clause

A relative clause is a type of subordinate clause. A relative clause is introduced by a relative adverb (such as 'when' or 'wherever') or a relative pronoun (such as 'which' or 'who').

Usually, a relative clause describes, or refers to, a noun or a noun phrase. For example, in the sentence 'The man who lives next door gave me some tomatoes', the relative clause 'who lives next door' describes 'the man'.

In some sentences, a relative clause can refer to a whole clause, rather than just the noun or noun phrase within it. For example, in the sentence 'Jack ate all of the cake, which upset the rest of the children', the relative clause 'which upset the rest of the children' refers not to 'Jack' or 'cake', but to the entire main clause 'Jack ate all of the cake'.

relative pronoun

A relative pronoun is a pronoun used to introduce a relative clause. For example, in the sentence 'The writer **whose** novel we are reading is very talented', the relative pronoun 'whose' introduces the relative clause 'whose novel we are reading'. Other relative pronouns include 'who', 'that', 'whom' and 'which'.

root word

A root word is the simplest form of word, the form without any prefixes or suffixes. A root word consists of a single morpheme, which cannot be split into smaller units. For example, 'kind' is the root of the longer word 'unkindness'.

round brackets

(see parentheses)

S

schwa

A schwa is an unstressed vowel sound, roughly equating to /uh/. The schwa has the lowest level of stress of any sound in spoken English.

The schwa is also the most common vowel sound in spoken English. It occurs when a vowel letter, which represents a clear, stressed vowel sound in most words, is instead sounded with an unstressed sound: for example, the ‹e› in 'children', which is pronounced as a schwa. Children can have difficulty spelling words in which a vowel is pronounced as a schwa, because they hear the /uh/ sound but are uncertain as to which vowel letter gives the correct spelling.

second person

In English, as in most languages, we have different personal pronouns for each of the different grammatical persons. The personal pronoun for the second person is 'you'. While most other grammatical persons have different personal pronouns for singular and plural, and for subject and object positions, this is not the case for the second person: the word 'you' is used in all cases. The second person pronoun denotes the addressee or addressees.

semantics

Semantics is the study of meaning. It is particularly concerned with the relationship between 'signifier' (a sign or a word) and 'signified' (the meaning of that sign or word). Semantics is a branch of linguistics.

semicolon

A semicolon (;) is used to join two main clauses that are closely related to each other: for example, 'Philip declined the fillet steak; he is a vegetarian' and 'James finds science difficult; however, he excels in art.' A semicolon is not used when the main clauses are already joined by a conjunction, as in the sentence 'Penny likes cabbage **but** Nadia hates it.'

Semicolons can also be used instead of commas to separate items in a complicated list. For example, if any of the items already has a comma, it is clearer to separate the list using semicolons, as in 'In the box there was an old, chipped cup; some Roman coins; and some torn, faded postcards'.

semivowel

A semivowel is a sound somewhere between a vowel and a consonant. For example, ‹y› acts as a consonant in the word '**y**ellow', but a vowel in the word 'funn**y**'. The letters ‹y› and ‹w› are technically considered to be semivowels.

sentence

A sentence is a group of words that begins with a capital letter, contains a subject and a verb, makes sense, and ends with a full stop, an exclamation mark or a question mark. A sentence must have at least one main clause, and may have one or more subordinate clauses.

A sentence can be simple, complex, compound, or compound-complex.

A simple sentence contains a single main clause: for example, 'The elephant ate the leaves from the tree.'

A complex sentence contains a main clause and at least one subordinate clause: for example, 'I drink lots of water because it is good for me.'

A compound sentence contains two or more main clauses, but no subordinate clauses: for example, 'Jane likes toast but Jonny hates it.'

Finally, a compound-complex sentence contains at least two main clauses and at least one subordinate clause: for example, 'While I looked for some new shoes, I saw this lovely dress and I bought it.'

sentence diagram

A sentence diagram is a visual representation of the structure of a sentence.

short vowel

The short vowel sounds are /a/ (as in 'cat'), /e/ (as in 'hen'), /i/ (as in 'sit'), /o/ (as in 'sock'), and /u/ (as in 'fun').

simple sentence

A simple sentence is a sentence

that contains just one main clause. The sentence 'The elephant ate the leaves from the tree' is simple because it has a single main clause and no subordinate clauses.

simple (verbs)

The simple tenses are used to talk about one-off actions (such as 'Albert **fell** over'), habitual actions (such as 'Ahmed **swims** every day'), or truths (such as 'Zebras **have** black and white stripes').

The simple present form of the verb is usually the same as the verb root, as in 'I **talk**' and 'You **rush**'. However, if the subject is in the third person singular, the third person singular marker (‹-s› or ‹-es›) is added, as in 'He **talks**' and 'She **rushes**'. The simple past tense of regular verbs is formed by adding the suffix ‹-ed› to the verb root, as in the sentence 'We **talked** yesterday.'

singular (nouns)

A singular noun refers to one of something. Most nouns have different forms for singular and plural. (This inflection is called declension.) The singular noun form is usually the same as the root form of the word.

singular pronouns

The singular pronouns are used to denote a single person. The first person singular ('I', 'me') is used when the speaker is referring to him, her or themself; the second person singular ('you', 'you') is used when the speaker is referring to the

addressee; and the third person singular ('he', 'she', 'they', 'it') is used to refer to someone else.

speech marks

Speech marks, also known as 'quotation marks' or 'inverted commas', look like this: " ". A pair of speech marks is used to separate direct speech (the spoken words of a person) from the rest of the sentence. When we quote direct speech in writing, we use opening speech marks (shaped like a '66') immediately before the spoken words and closing speech marks (shaped like a '99') afterwards. It is important to quote the spoken words in between the speech marks exactly as they were said: for example, '"I'm tired," said Tim.'

Speech marks are only used for direct speech; reported speech (as in 'Tim said that he was tired.') does not require speech marks.

split digraph

A split digraph (also known as a 'hop-over ‹e›' or 'magic ‹e›' digraph) is a vowel digraph whose two letters have been separated by a consonant letter: for example, the ‹a_e› in 'm**a**k**e**' and the ‹i_e› in 'f**i**n**e**'.

Split digraphs usually make the long vowel sound of the first vowel letter; the second vowel letter (often an ‹e›) is usually silent. However, there are some exceptions. In the word 't**o**tal' the second vowel ‹a› affects the sound made by the first vowel ‹o›, turning it from a short vowel into a long vowel, as well as saying its own sound.

square brackets

A pair of square brackets (**[ ]**) are used to indicate that some text (which could be a sentence, a phrase, a word or even a single letter) has been inserted into, or deleted from, a direct quotation.

We use an opening square bracket immediately before any inserted text and a closing square bracket immediately afterwards, as in the sentence, '[He] loathe[s] vegetables.' Here, the square brackets show that the third person singular marker has been added by the writer, but was not part of the original quotation (which would have been 'I loathe vegetables').

When words have been omitted from a direct quotation (ellipsis), we indicate where the words were with three dots within a pair of square brackets, as in the sentence 'According to the most recent data, "young children **[...]** learn better in a secure environment."'

Standard English

Dialects are typically classed as 'standard' or 'non-standard'. For example, 'I **done** my homework' would be classed as non-standard English, while 'I **have done** my homework' (or 'I **did** my homework') would be classed as Standard English.

Standard English is the dialect that has been established as the universal norm and, as such, it is the dialect used for formal spoken and written communication.

statement

A statement is a sentence that is used to assert something as being the case. A statement is either true or false. A statement is made using a declarative sentence: for example, 'Mo is my brother' or 'The dog ate my lunch.' We usually use a full stop at the end of a statement.

stem

A stem is the part of a word that remains the same in all of the inflected forms. A word's stem can be the same as its root: for example, the stem of the word 'strongest' is the root word 'strong'; or it can be more complex: for example, the stem of the word 'sleepwalking' is 'sleepwalk'.

stress

Stress refers to the amount of emphasis given to a particular syllable within a word, or to a particular word within a sentence.

Stress can have an effect on meaning. Stressing different words in a sentence can modify or clarify the meaning of that sentence. For example, 'I saw him' could variously mean '**I** saw him' ('It was me that did the seeing'); 'I **saw** him' ('I really did see him'); or 'I saw **him**' ('It was this particular male that I saw').

Occasionally, two different words are only distinguishable by their different stress patterns: for example 'de**sert**' (a noun denoting an area that has little or no rain) and 'de**sert**' (a verb meaning 'abandon').

subject

In a sentence, the subject is the noun or pronoun that 'does' the verb action. Every complete sentence has a subject. For example, the subject of the sentence 'Jack bought pasta' is 'Jack': he is the person that does the buying.

subject pronoun

Pronouns are the little words used to replace nouns. The subject pronouns are as follows: 'I', 'you', 'he', 'she', 'it', 'we', 'you' and 'they'. These pronouns are used as the subject of a sentence: for example, '**I** like this dog'; '**She** gave the book to Bob'; '**He** sat on the floor.'

subjunctive

The subjunctive mood is a type of irrealis mood. It is used when talking about wishes, possibilities, opinions, suggestions or desires. For example, in the sentence 'I propose that James be promoted', James's promotion is not a fact, but a proposition: it might, or might not, take place.

subordinate clause

A subordinate (or 'dependent') clause is a type of clause that cannot stand as a complete sentence by itself. Instead, it must be used together with a main clause as part of a complex (or compound-complex) sentence. For example, the subordinate clause 'While he was at the bank' does not work as a complete sentence by itself. We are left wondering what happened while he was at the bank. It is only when it is used with a main clause that it forms a complete sentence, as in the complex sentence 'While he was at the bank, I bought some shoes.'

There are a number of different types of subordinate clauses, including relative clauses (such as 'The man **who lives next door** gave me some tomatoes'), adverbial clauses (such as '**When I have finished my book**, I will go for a run'), complement clauses (such as 'I am certain **that the Earth is a sphere**'), and embedded questions (such as 'I don't know **where the dictionaries are**').

subordinating conjunction

A subordinating conjunction is a word that joins the main clause in a sentence to a subordinate one. For example, the word 'while' in the sentence 'While he was at the bank, I bought some shoes' is a subordinating conjunction. Other common subordinating conjunctions are 'whereas', 'though', 'whenever', 'when', 'before', 'after', 'although' and 'because'.

subordination

Subordination describes an unequal relationship between clauses or words. A subordinate clause is subordinate (inferior) to the main clause, or word, that it modifies. For example, in the sentence 'Jack ate all of the cake, which upset the rest of the children', the relative clause 'which upset the rest of the children' is subordinate to the main clause 'Jack ate all of the cake.' Similarly, in the sentence 'I am certain that the Earth is a sphere', the complement clause 'that the Earth is a sphere' is subordinate to the adjective 'certain'.

Within a clause certain words are subordinate to other words. Adjectives, for example, are subordinate to the noun or pronoun that they describe.

suffix

A suffix is a morpheme (usually one or more syllables) that is added to the end of a word to add to, or change, its meaning. For example, when the suffix ‹-less› is added to the word 'hope', the resulting word, 'hope**less**', means 'without hope'. In contrast, when the suffix ‹-ful› is added to the word 'hope', the resulting word, 'hope**ful**', means 'full of hope'.

Suffixes can also affect the part of speech of a word. When the suffix ‹-ly› is added to certain adjectives, the resulting words are adverbs: for example, 'slow**ly**', 'carefull**y**' and 'safe**ly**'. Similarly, when the suffix ‹-y› is added to certain nouns, the resulting words are adjectives: for example, 'mess**y**', 'cloud**y**' and 'rust**y**'. Suffixes are also added to verbs to show tense and subject: for example, the suffix ‹-ed› is added to a verb to indicate the simple past tense, as in 'walk**ed**', 'seem**ed**' and 'play**ed**'. Similarly, the suffix ‹-s› (or ‹-es›) can be added to a singular noun to make its plural: for example, 'cat' becomes 'cat**s**' in the plural.

superlative adjective

A superlative adjective describes a noun or a pronoun by comparing it with the rest of the items in a group to which that noun or pronoun also belongs. For example, in the sentence 'Fred is the **youngest** boy in the team', the superlative adjective 'youngest' describes 'Fred' by comparing him with the rest of the members of his team.

Superlatives can be formed by adding the suffix ‹-est› to the positive adjective (as in 'young**est**' or 'long**est**'), or by using the word 'most' before the positive adjective (as in '**most** difficult' or '**most** careful').

syllable

A syllable is a unit of sound that contains a vowel sound. A syllable can either form part of a word (such as the 'scoo' of '**scoo**ter'), or constitute a whole word by itself (as in the monosyllabic word 'boat').

synonym

A synonym is a word or phrase whose meaning is the same as (or similar to) that of another word or phrase. For example, the words 'declared', 'stated' and 'proclaimed' are synonyms.

See also antonym.

syntax

Syntax is the branch of linguistics that is particularly concerned with the study of sentence structure.

synthesising

(see blending)

synthetic phonics

Synthetic phonics is a method of teaching reading and writing. Teachers using a synthetic phonics approach begin by introducing the letters (and digraphs) and their corresponding sounds. Once the children know enough letter sounds to make a word, they are taught how to blend the sounds together to read words. Jolly Phonics is a synthetic phonics programme.

T

tense (verbs)

A verb's tense indicates when the action, event, state or change that is denoted by the verb takes place.

Technically, the English language has only two tenses: the past and the present. The past tense is usually used when talking about something that has already taken place. The present tense is usually used when talking about something that has not already taken place: typically something that is taking place now, or is relevant to the time of speaking. To talk about the future, we usually use the present tense form of a verb together with the auxiliary verb 'will' (or 'shall'), as in 'We **shall talk** tomorrow.' Although this formation does not, strictly speaking, constitute a distinct tense, it can be helpful to talk about verbs as happening in the past, the present or the future.

Verbs are inflected for tense. With regular verbs, the simple past tense is formed by adding the suffix ‹-ed› to the verb root, as in the sentence 'We **talked** for an hour.' The simple present tense form of the verb is usually the same as the verb root, as in 'We **talk** every day.'

In the continuous aspect, the present and past tenses are formed with the auxiliary verb 'to be' (in the present or past tense) and the present participle, as in the sentences 'We **are talking** right now' (present), and 'We **were talking** a few moments ago' (past).

In the perfect aspect, the present and past tenses are formed with the auxiliary verb 'to have' (in the present or past tense) and the past participle, as in the sentences 'We **have talked** already' (present), and 'We **had talked** previously' (past).

Tense and aspect are often conflated and, for simplicity, we avoid using the term 'grammatical aspect' when teaching children about verbs and verb tenses in the Jolly Phonics grammar programme. Instead, we refer to the various tenses in the continuous aspect as the 'continuous tenses', and the various tenses in the perfect aspect as the 'perfect tenses'.

See also past tense, present tense and aspect.

third person

In English, as in most languages, we have different personal pronouns for each of the different grammatical persons.

The personal pronouns for the third person singular are 'he', 'him', 'she', 'her', 'they', 'them' and 'it', and for the third person plural they are 'they' and 'them'.

The third person singular is used to refer to someone other than the speaker (or writer) and their addressee. The third person plural is used to refer to more than one other person.

In the third person, the personal pronouns we use are affected by gender. So we use the words 'he' and 'him' for the masculine, 'she' and 'her' for the feminine, 'they' and 'them' for the non-gender specific and 'it' for the neuter.

third person singular marker

The third person singular marker is an ‹-s› (or ‹-es›) that is added to the end of a regular verb in the simple present tense when the subject is in the third person singular. For example, we say 'I **talk**' but 'He **talks**', and 'You **rush**' but 'She **rushes**'.

transitive verb

A transitive verb is a verb that takes a direct object. Some verbs are always transitive and make no sense without an object: for example, the verb 'to want'. 'Jim wants' cannot be considered a complete sentence by itself. We are left wondering what Jim wants. It is only when a direct object is added that it forms a complete sentence, as in 'Jim wants **a cup of tea**.'

Other verbs can be transitive or intransitive depending on the context: for example, in the sentence 'She opens her present', the verb 'to open' is transitive, taking 'present' as its direct object; however, in the sentence 'The door opens with a creak', the verb 'to open' is intransitive.

See also intransitive verb.

tricky word

A tricky word is a frequently used word with an irregular spelling, for example 'other', which cannot be read simply by blending together the sounds that its component letters most commonly represent. Tricky words are read by blending the regular part(s) of the word, in this case /th/ and /er/, and learning the 'tricky' part, in this case the ‹o›, which is pronounced with an /u/ sound.

trigraph

A trigraph is a set of three letters that, together, represent a single sound. For example, the /ie/ sound in the word 'light' is written with three letters: ‹igh›.

U

uncountable noun

Uncountable nouns (also known as 'mass' or 'non-count' nouns) denote substances, (such as 'mud', 'water', 'metal' and 'air') or abstract concepts (such as 'intelligence', 'music', 'news' and 'peace'), neither of which can be divided into discrete 'countable' units. Uncountable nouns cannot usually be used with an indefinite article ('a' or 'an'), or directly modified by a numeral. So while we can say '**a** dog' and '**twelve** cats', we cannot usually say '**a** mud' or '**twelve** waters'. In order to use an indefinite article or a numeral with an uncountable noun, we first have to specify a certain amount of the substance: for example, 'a **bucket of** mud' or 'twelve **gallons of** water'.

However, in certain contexts, some uncountable nouns can function as countable nouns. When uncountable nouns are used as countable nouns, they usually denote more than one instance of a particular type of substance. For example, in the sentence 'Most **metals** are solid at room temperature' the word 'metal', which is usually an uncountable noun, is acting as a countable noun and means 'types of metal'.

When talking about a smaller amount of an uncountable noun we usually use the word 'less', as in '**less** flour' or '**less** water'. In contrast, when talking about a smaller number of countable nouns we usually use the word 'fewer', as in '**fewer** cats'.

unstressed

Stress refers to the amount of emphasis given to a particular syllable within a word, or to a particular word within a sentence.

Unstressed syllables or words are given less emphasis than stressed ones. The schwa, an unstressed vowel sound, has the lowest level of stress of any sound in spoken English.

V

verb

A verb denotes what a person or thing does and can describe an action, an event, a state or a change.

On the most basic level, verbs can be divided into **lexical** (or 'main') verbs, such as 'run', 'play', 'jump' and 'sing', and **auxiliary** (or 'helping') verbs, such as 'should', 'must', 'will' and 'can'. Lexical verbs can be further divided into **transitive** verbs (which require a direct object), **intransitive** verbs (which do not require a direct object), and **linking** verbs (which connect the subject to its predicate). Every complete sentence must have at least one lexical verb.

The form of the verb that we

use in a sentence is inflected (changed) to agree with its subject. For example, we would say 'I **like** flowers', but 'She **likes** flowers'. In the second sentence, the third person singular marker (‹-s›) has been added to the verb 'like' so that it agrees with the third person singular subject 'she'.

A verb's form also changes to indicate its aspect, tense and mood. For example, in the sentence 'I **had eaten** already', the verb form is inflected for the perfect aspect, the past tense and the indicative mood.

See also finite verb, intransitive verb, lexical verb, linking verb, phrasal verb and transitive verb.

vowel

The five vowel letters are ‹a›, ‹e›, ‹i›, ‹o› and ‹u›. These letters correspond to the five short vowel sounds: /a/ (as in 'cat'), /e/ (as in 'hen'), /i/ (as in 'sit'), /o/ (as in 'sock') and /u/ (as in 'fun').

As well as the five short vowel sounds, English also has five long vowel sounds: /ai/ (as in 'train'), /ee/ (as in 'tree'), /ie/ (as in 'cried'), /oa/ (as in 'toad'), and /ue/ (as in 'cue'). These sounds are the same as the names of the five vowel letters: ‹A›, ‹E›, ‹I›, ‹O› and ‹U›.

Other vowel sounds include /or/ (as in 'horse'), the little and long /oo/ sounds (as in 'look' and 'moon'), /ou/ (as in 'house'), /oi/ (as in 'boil'), /er/ (as in 'verb'), /ar/ (as in 'car'), /ear/ (as in 'fear'), and /air/ (as in 'fair'). The letter ‹y› also makes a vowel sound in some words, such as 'happy', 'myth' and 'fly'.

Technically, a vowel sound is made with an open vocal tract. In contrast, a consonant sound is made when the lips, throat, teeth or tongue partially, or completely, prevent the air from flowing through the vocal tract.

W X Y Z

word

A word is the smallest linguistic unit that has meaning and can stand alone. Some words, such as 'kind', consist of a single morpheme, but other words contain more than one morpheme. 'Unkindness', for example, has three morphemes: 'un-', 'kind' and '-ness'. All three of these morphemes contribute to the meaning of the whole word, but only the root word, 'kind', can stand alone.

Unlike morphemes, all words can stand alone and convey a meaning.

word class

(see part of speech)

word family

A word family is a set of words that are connected by a shared root word. For example, the words 'kind', 'unkind', 'kindly', 'unkindly', 'kindness' and 'unkindness' are all part of the same word family.

Parts of Speech Actions

common noun

Touch your forehead with your
index and middle fingers.

proper noun

Touch your forehead with your
index and middle finger.

concrete noun

Gently tap your forehead
twice with your hand.

abstract noun

Move your hand away from your
forehead in a spiral action.

first person singular

(I, me, mine)
Point to yourself.

second person singular

(you, yours)
Point to someone else.

third person singular

(she, her, hers)
Point to a girl.

third person singular

(he, him, his)
Point to a boy.

third person singular

(it, its)
Point to the floor.

first person plural

(we, us, ours) Point in a circle
to yourself and others.

second person plural

(you, yours)
Point to two other people.

third person plural

(they, them, their)
Point to the class next door.

verb

Clench both fists and move your
arms backwards and forwards
at your sides, as if running.

past tense verbs

Point backwards over your
shoulder with your thumb.

present tense verbs

Point towards the floor with
the palm of your hand.

future verbs

Point towards the front
(with your finger).

adjective

Touch the side of your temple with your fist.

adverb

Bang one fist on top of the other.

conjunction

Hold your hands apart with the palms facing up and move them, so one is on top of the other.

preposition

Point from one noun to another.

definite article

Make a capital T with your hands, with one hand facing palm down and the other pointing up towards it.

indefinite article

Hold up your hand, palm facing forwards, and point to your thumb.